German shepherds are strong, hard-working dogs

German Shepherds

Jean Allen

A⁺

Smart Apple Media

COPYRIGHT

Published by Smart Apple Media

1980 Lookout Drive, North Mankato, MN 56003

Designed by Rita Marshall

Printed in the United States of America

Photographs by Barbara Augello, Joan Balzarini, Corbis (Robert Llewellyn),
dogpix.com (Larry Reynolds), Sally Myers, Tom Myers, Unicorn Stock Photos
(Marie Mills, Gary Randall, Dick Young)

Library of Congress Cataloging-in-Publication Data

Allen, Jean. German shepherds / by Jean Allen.

p. cm. – (Dog breeds) Summary: Introduces the physical characteristics,
life cycle, breeding, training, and care of German shepherds.

ISBN 1-58340-313-2

1. German shepherd dog–Juvenile literature. [1. German shepherd dog.
2. Dogs.] I. Title. II. Series.

SF429.G37L64 2003   636.737'6–dc21   2002042809

First Edition 9 8 7 6 5 4 3 2 1

German Shepherds

CONTENTS

Working Dogs

Several police officers are stepping slowly through the woods. The leaves and branches are so thick that the officers can hardly see. A large dog walks ahead of them, sniffing the ground. Suddenly, the dog barks and runs toward a large tree. There, huddled against the tree trunk, is a young boy who had wandered away from his family's campsite. The dog is a German shepherd, and it just helped rescue a lost child.

German shepherds are smart, loyal animals. They have good

A medal-winning German shepherd police dog

hearing, eyesight, and sense of smell. They are easy to train and take commands very well. That is why dogs of this **breed** are often trained to be working dogs. Working dogs can do many different jobs. German shepherd police dogs help find missing people. They also sniff out hidden bombs, guns, and drugs. German shepherd service dogs can be trained to open doors, bring a phone to their owners, or lead blind people safely across the street.

A German shepherd's nose works so well that it can sometimes smell things a half-mile (.8 km) away!

A German shepherd trained to carry rescue tools

Thick coats keep German shepherds warm

German shepherds can also be sheepherders. They guard the

sheep and warn people if the sheep are in danger.

German Shepherd Basics

German shepherds are usually black and tan, but they can also be black, gray, or white. Their thick coats keep moisture out and

The first German shepherd recognized by the American Kennel Club, in 1908, was known as a "German sheepdog."

warmth in. In many parts of the world, German shepherds live

outdoors year-round. German shepherds are larger than

most dogs. Males stand 24 to 26 inches (61–66 cm) tall from

the tops of their shoulders to the ground. They weigh 70 to 90

pounds (32–41 kg). Females are usually a few inches shorter

and weigh about 20 pounds (9 kg) less. 🐕 Female German

German shepherds come in a mix of colors

shepherds give birth to **litters** of two to six pups. For the first few weeks, puppies spend all of their time eating and sleeping. By the time they are 8 to 10 weeks old, puppies are ready to be **weaned**. They are also ready to start training. German shepherds are full-grown at nine months. With good care, they can live about 10 years.

The First German Shepherd

The first German shepherd was raised in Germany around 1900. Captain Max von Stephanitz was a military officer and an expert on dogs. He wanted to raise a dog that

was the best sheeperder ever.  Throughout the 1890s, von

Stephanitz studied dogs and went to dog shows. Finally, in

1899, he found exactly what he was looking for at a small dog

A seven-week-old German shepherd puppy

show in England. This dog was both **obedient** and lively. The

dog was named Horand, and it was recognized as the first

German shepherd dog. A few years later, the breed came

to America and then spread around the world. According to the American Kennel Club, the German shepherd is now the third most popular dog breed in the United States. Only the Labrador retriever and the golden retriever are more popular.

Today, more than 51,000 German shepherd dogs are listed with the American Kennel Club.

German shepherds are popular pets

German Shepherds as Pets

German shepherds are strong, hard-working dogs, but they also make excellent pets. They are eager to please and love to run and play. Before choosing a German shepherd puppy, it is important to watch how it behaves. Some puppies are bossy and can be hard to train. The best puppy is strong and happy and gets along with other dogs. German shepherds need a lot of exercise. They should be walked at least two times a day, for about 20 minutes each time. More exercise would be even better. Food, water, and **grooming** are

also important in caring for a German shepherd. High-quality

dog food has a lot of meat in it and will help keep a

German shepherd healthy. The dog should also have fresh

Playful German shepherd pups

water available at all times. Owners should brush their German shepherd at least once a week and keep the dog's toenails trimmed. Regular visits to the **veterinarian** are important, too. All dogs need shots to keep them from getting sick. German shepherds are raised to do important jobs, but they can also make great pets. With

The first Seeing Eye dogs were German shepherds. They helped blind soldiers in Germany after World War I.

good care—and lots of love—a German shepherd can be a wonderful friend for many years.

A young, well-groomed German shepherd

Training and Teamwork

Well-trained German shepherds know many different commands. Get together with a friend and take turns pretending to be a dog and its handler (the person the dog is supposed to obey). Remember, the dog and its handler are a team!

If you are the handler, say your command just once, in a firm voice. Say "good" and the dog's name when the dog does the right thing. Say "no" when the dog does something wrong. Do not punish the dog for mistakes.

Heel—the dog should walk with its shoulder next to the handler's leg.

Sit—the dog should sit.

Stay—the dog should not move until the handler gives another command.

Down—the dog should lie down on its belly.

Fetch—the dog should get an object and bring it back to the handler.

Come or **Here**—the dog should go to the handler.

Hup—the dog should jump.

German shepherds can be trained to fetch sticks

Index

Words to Know

breed (BREED)—a type of dog, such as a poodle, collie, or bulldog

grooming (GROOM-ing)—brushing and cleaning

litters (LITT-urz)—groups of puppies born at the same time

obedient (oh-BEE-dee-ent)—well behaved; follows directions

veterinarian (VET-ur-eh-NAIR-ee-en)—a doctor for animals

weaned (WEEND)—when a puppy stops drinking its mother's milk and starts eating other foods

Read More

Kallen, Stuart A. *German Shepherds*. New York: Checkerboard Library, 1996.

Stone, Lynn M. *German Shepherds*. Vero Beach, Fla.: The Rourke Book Company, 2002.

Wilcox, Charlotte. *The German Shepherd*. Mankato, Minn.: Capstone Press, 1996.

Internet Sites

American Kennel Club: German Shepherd Dog
http://www.akc.org/breeds/recbreeds/germshep.cfm

Dog Owner's Guide
http://www.canismajor.com/dog

FBI: Working Dogs
http://www.fbi.gov/kids/dogs/doghome.htm

Germanshepherds.com
http://www.germanshepherds.com

INFORMATION